ॐ शान्तिः शान्तिः शा

THE SANSKRIT ALPHABET

The Sanskrit alphabet is organized as follows, reading from left to right:

Vowels (when not combined with consonants)

अ a　आ ā　इ i　ई ī　उ u　ऊ ū

ऋ ṛ　ॠ ṝ　ऌ ḷ

ए e　ओ o　ऐ ai　औ au

Consonants (with inherent vowel *a*)

Velar:　　क ka　ख kha　ग ga　घ gha　ङ ṅa
Palatals:　च ca　छ cha　ज ja　झ jha　ञ ña
Cerebrals:　ट ṭa　ठ ṭha　ड ḍa　ढ ḍha　ण ṇa
Dentals:　त ta　थ tha　द da　ध dha　न na
Labials:　प pa　फ pha　ब ba　भ bha　म ma
Semivowels:　य ya　र ra　ल la　व va
Sibilants:　श śa　ष ṣa　स sa
Aspirate:　ह ha

(Add-on signs:)　ṁ (anusvāra)　ḥ (visarga)

PART 1: BABY GIRL NAMES

Abdhi	A pond, lake, ocean; Sea of milk
Abha	Splendor; Light; Precious
Abhati	Shines, Illumines
Abheda	Non-difference
Abhidhā	To give; Bestow for a purpose; Power of a word; Praise
Abhidhyai	To consider; Reflect; Meditate upon
Abhigna	Knowledgeable; knowing; Skillful; Clever
Abhignāya	Having recognized; Having remembered
Abhijiti	Victory; Conquest
Abhijna	Direction; perception or recollection assisted by memory
Abhikānkshā	Longing; Wish; Desire
Abhikhyā	Look; View; Splendor; Beauty; Gracious
Abhilāshini	Wishing; Desiring; Desirous; Covetous
Abhilipsā	Desire of obtaining
Abhinandini	Rejoicing at; Wishing; Desiring

Abhinandita	Delighted; Made happy; Saluted; Applauded
Abhinaya	Performance; Passion; Gesture; Dramatic personification
Abhinaya	Controlling; training; disciplining
Abhiniti	Gesture; Expressive gesticulation; Friendship; Civility; Kindness
Abhinivesa	Clinging to earthly life; will to live
Abhinivistha	Well versed; Proficient; Conversant; Familiar; Endowed with
Abhiprāpti	Reaching; Obtaining; Arrival
Abhiprīti	Rejoicing in; Wish; Desire
Abhipsini	Desirous of obtaining; Wishing
Abhipsu	Desirous of obtaining; Wishing
Abhishri	Respected; Shining; Powerful; Joining; Connecting one's self with
Abhishtā	Wished; Desired; Acceptable; Dear; Favourate; Darling
Abhīti	Fearlessness
Abja	Lotus flower; The Moon
Abjini	Possessing lotus flowers; The Sun
Achala	Not moving; fixed

Adhā	Auspicious; Inceptive particle
Adhiti	Perusal; Study; Desire; Recollection
Adhokshaja	A being who cannot be perceived by the outer senses; a name of Bhagavan Narayana
Adhya	Jewel; Wealthy
Aditi	Freedom; Sincerity; Safety; Boundlessness; Immensity; Perfection; Divinity
Adrishta	The unseen principle
Advaita	Non-duality; monism
Advayā	Unique; Only; Without second; Name of Buddha; Ultimate truth
Advesha	Not malevolent; Without opposition; Not to be disliked
Advitiya	Without a second
Adya	Primordial; original
Agadha	Deep; Unfathomable; not shallow
Agama	The Veda; manual of practical worship; profound
Agami	Karma now produced, to be enjoyed after
Agati	Stability
Aghrini	Radiant

Agni-hotri	A fire offering
Ahalya	Wife of sage Gautama
Ahuti	Oblation (poured into the fire in sacrifices)
Aisa	Devine; Supreme; Epithet of lord Shiva
Aisvarya	Material or spiritual wealth
Ajani	Path; Way; Road
Ajīti	Un-fadingness; Freedom from decay; Prosperity
Akalpa	Ornament
Akanksha	Wish
Akhila	Complete; Whole; Without a gap
Aksh	To reach; Pass through; Pervade; Embrace; Accumulate
Aksha	The eye; Organ of sense; A substitute for Akshi
Akshara	Imperishable; Unalterable; Lord Shiva; Lord Vishnu; Brahma
Akshara	Imperishable
Akshata	Unblemished maiden; A virgin
Akshaya	Un-decaying; Imperishableness

Akshaya	Un-decaying
Akshita	Imperishable
Akshiti	Imperishableness; Imperishable
Akshiti	Imperishableness
Aktā	The night
Akurcha	Guileless; Genuine
Alini	Life, Ruler, Bee
Alokya	Extraordinary
Amala	Spotless; Stainless; Clean; Pure; Shining; White
Amani	A way; Wish
Amaravati	The adobe of immortals; Capital of Indra
Amaya	Free from error or deceit; Absence of dilution or guile
Ambhikā	Name of goddess Parvati; Wife of lord Shiva
Ambika	Name of goddess Parvathi; Mother
Ambuja	Lotus flower; Name of goddess Lakshmi
Amisha	Luxury; Object of enjoyment, flesh

Amisha	Honesty; Simplicity
Amita	Boundless; Infinite; Unmeasured
Amita	Infinite; Boundless
Amithyā	Not falsely; Truthfully
Amrita	Immortal; Imperishable; Beautiful; Beloved; Desired
Amūdha	Not Infatuated; Not perplexed; Wise
Amulya	Invaluable; Priceless
Amūlya	Priceless; Not to be purchased
Amurt	Without form
Amurta	Without form
Anagha	Innocent; Sinless; Faultless; Handsome; Epithet of Shiva
Anamya	Unbendable
Ananya	Unique; Only; Without second; Sole; Not more than one
Anasya	Indestructible
Anchati	Wind; Fire
Anchita	Reverenced; Honoured; Distinguished; Curved

Anhiti	Gift; Donation
Anima	Subtlety; the power of making the body subtle
Animisha	Absence of winking; Vigilantly; Incessantly; Related to Gods
Anisha	Uninterrupted; Incessant; Night less; Related to God
Anjali	Reverence; Salutation; Benediction
Anjani	Name of Mother of Hanuman; Name of Mountain
Ankitā	Marked; Numbered; Counted; Calculated
Ansha	Part; Portion; Inheritance; Earnest money; Name of Aditya
Anu	Fine; Minute; Atomic; An atom of time; An atom matter; Name of Shiva
Anubha	Lightening
Anubhā	Lightening
Anūdita	Spoken after; Spoken according to
Anugnā	To permit; Grant; Allow; To entreat; Behave kindly
Anuhā	To grant
Anūja	Young; Younger sister
Anūkti	Mentioning after; Repeated mention; Study of the Veda

Anumā	Conclusion; Inference
Anūna	Whole; Entire; Having full power; Not inferior; Name of an Apsaras.
Anunaya	Kind; Tenderly
Anunīti	Conciliation; Courtesy; Supplication
Anupama	Incomparable; Matchless; Excellent; Best
Anusmriti	Cherished recollection; Recalling idea
Anusri	Follow; To pursue
Anusriti	Going after; Following; Confirming to
Anuyā	Follow; Attend; To take
Anvānī	To lead to; To lead along
Anvaya	Following; Succession; Logical connection of cause and effect
Anvaya	Direct, positive, co-existence; the natural connection of words in a sentence
Anvikshā	Reflection; Meditation; Searching
Anvikshana	Reflection; Meditation; Searching
Anvistha	Sought; Required

Anvita	Joined; Connected; Essential or inherent part; Endowed; Possessed; Understood
Anviti	Following after; Food
Anyatha	Separateness; the state of being otherwise
Aparajita	Unconquerable
Aparna	Name of Durga; Parvati
Apeksha	Desire; Having regarded to
Apekshita	Relative
Aprajnata	Unknown
Aprameya	Immeasurable
Apta	Competent person; a sage or an adept; a well-wisher
Apurva	Unseen; strange; extraordinary; the hidden power
Apūva	Quite new; unprecedented; Not having existed before
Aradhana	Respectable worship of God; special adoration
Arati	Divine service performed to God
Aravindinī	An assemblage of lotus flowers
Archana	Worship; Praising; Celebrating

Archana	Offering of flowers and sacred leaves
Architri	Worshiper
Argha	worship; Reverence; Worthy
Arghya	Offering of water to Devatas and Rishis
Arhanā	Worship; Adoration; Honour; Respect
Arka	A ray of light; A sun beam
Arkinī	Shining; Praising
Arpana	Offering to god; Sacrifice
Arthagna	Generous; Liberal; Bountiful
Arūkshana	Soft; Tender
Arundhati	Wife of sage Vishwamitra; Asterism
Arunimā	Redness; Ruddiness
Arunita	Bright red; Bright like Sun
Arusha	A dark red cloud; Tawny
Asa	Hope; expectation
Ashvini	A Star; Deity

Atishthā	To excel; Precedence; Superiority
Atmaja	Goddess Parvathi
Atmaja	Durga; Daughter
Atmasrayi	Dependent on the Self for existence, as the case of Isvara
Atmika	Soul; Atman; Passionate
Atulya	Unequalled; Surpassing
Aushija	Desirous; Sunrise
Avani	The Earth
Avijnata	Unknown; Brahma
Aya	Good luck; Favourable fortune
Ayana	Road; Path; Going; Course; Period; Final emancipation
Ayana	Movement; the sun's passage
Ayāsya	Not to be obtained by effort; Indefatigable; Valiant; Enterprising
Ayati	Dignity
Ayoga	Made of flowers
Ayuta	Undisturbed; Inseparable

Ibha	An elephant; Ruler
Ibhyā	Wealthy
Ilā	The Earth; Flow; Speech
Inakshati	Desire; Endeavour; Goal
Indirā	An epithet of goddess Lakshmi
Indrani	Wife of Indra; Goddess Durga; Devine energy
Indu	The Moon; Spark
Irā	Water; Name of an Apsarasa
Ish	A desirable object; Comfort
Ishā	Servant of Lord Shiva
Ishāna	An epithet of Durga; Light; Splendor
Ishika	Reed; Rush; Stem or stalk of grasses; An arrow; Eye ball of elephant
Ishira	Vigorous, active, refresh
Ishira	Vigorous; Active; Refresh
Ishta	Object of desire; the chosen ideal; the particular form of God
Ishti	Wish

Ishu	An arrow
Iva	Like; In some way
Iyakshu	Desire; Seeking
Udaya	Rise of Sun; Ascend; Prosperity
Udvi	To look up; To consider
Uma	Wife of lord Shiva
Upasana	Worship; Respect; Adoration
Upasana	Sitting near; worship or contemplation of God or deity; devout meditation
Upasita	Worship; Honor
Upasya	Worship; Respect; Regard
Upasya	Fit to be worshipped
Urmi	A wave; an evil; reference is often made to six evils (hunger and thirst, old age and death, grief and delusion or loss of consciousness)
Urvasi	Wish; Desire
Usha	Shine; Brilliant; Morning light
Ekayana	Union of thoughts; monotheism

Ekta	Oneness; homogeneity; absoluteness
Esha	An epithet of Lord Vishnu; Desire
Kalki	Lord Vishnu 10th incarnation
Kalpana	Design; Idea; Making; Fixing; Decorating
Kalpana	Imagination of the mind; creation
Kalpanika	That which is imagined; falsely created
Kalyani	Beautiful, Agreeable, Friendly, Noble
Kalyani	Auspicious; blessed
Kamala	Desire, Lotus, Goddess Lakshmi, Lord Brahma
Kamalini	Lotus flower; Assemblage of lotus flowers
Kamna	Longing; pleasure-seeking
Karuna	Mercy; compassion; kindness
Kavitri	Wise; Learned
Kavya	Prophetic; Poetic; Inspired; Wise; Intelligent
Ketu	Bright; Light; Leader; Intelligent
Khyati	Reputation; fame; knowledge

Khyāti	Glory; Fame; Renown
Kirtana	Singing the name and glory of God
Kīrtana	Recite; Prayer; Praising; Repeating
Kirti	Fame; reputation
Kīrti	Glory; Fame
Komala	Tender; Beautiful; Soft; Pleasing
Komya	Love; Quick thinker; Ruler
Kripā	Mercy; Compassion; Tenderness
Kripanya	Wish; Desire
Krisānga	Lord Shiva
Krisānu	Devine; God; Rudra
Kriti	Creation; Composition; Enchantment
Krittika	Constellation; Fire; Moon
Kshiti	Earth
Kshoni	The Earth
Kuhu	Moon; River

Kunalika	Indian Cuckoo; Kokila
Kunda	Jasmine flower
Kundini	Assemblage of Jasmin or Lotus flowers
Kusuma	Flower; Fruit; A form of fire
Kusumanjali	Handful of flowers
Kusumita	Decorated with flowers
Garima	A power of Yogi; one of the eight major Siddhis
Gauri	Goddess Parvathi
Gayatri	Sacred verses; Sacred Hymns; Goddess; The Sun
Gita	Song; conventionally refers to sacred text Bhagavad Gita
Gītika	Short Song; Short Hymn
Gnanamayi	Full of knowledge
Gnanasphurti	Flash of knowledge
Gneya	Knowable; to be known
Gomati	River; Owner of cow herd
Gritsa	Clever; Dexterous; Judicious; Wise

Gunamayi	Full of qualities or attributes
Chaitanyamayi	Full of consciousness
Chakshani	Eye; Radiating; Illuminating
Chakshu	Eye; Prince
Chamundi	Durga
Chanda	Epithet of Durga; Epithet of Shiva; Passionate; Fierce
Chandana	Sandal; Devine; Prince; River
Chandi	Goddess Durga
Chandita	Gratified; Pleasing
Chandrima	Moon light
Charanamrita	Water sanctified by the feet of a deity
Charita	Story; Nature; Practiced; Acts; Deeds
Charusheela	Beautiful, Jewel, Offering; Epithet of Shiva
Chauksha	Pure; Honest; Clever; Delightful; Beautiful
Chinmaya	Intelligence; Thought; Mind; Soul
Chinmayi	Full of Consciousness

Chiti	Knowing; Understanding; Thinking mind
Chitrangada	Decorated with brilliant or variegated bracelet
Choksha	Pure; Honest; Clever; Delightful; Beautiful
Citra	Bright; Visible; Distinguished
Jahnavi	River Ganga;
Jahnu	King, Sage who adopted Ganga as daughter
Jaladhija	Ocean-born; Goddess Lakshmi
Jalāsha	Pleasing; Healing; Comforting
Janani	Mother; Birth
Jaya	Victory; Winning
Jaya	Victory; mastery
Jayati	Victory; Winning; Excel
Jenya	Noble; Genuine; True wealth; Epithet of Indra, Agni
Jesha	Gaining; Winning; Excelling
Jigisha	Desire to conquer; Wish to Excel
Jigyu	Victorious

Joshna	Happiness; Satisfaction; Enjoyment; Approval
Joshya	Delightful; Agreeable; Welcome
Juhu	Tongue; Epithet of Agni; Flame
Jurni	Glowing fire; Blaze; The Sun; The Brahma
Jushti	Love; Service; Satisfaction
Jushya	Love; Worship
Jvala	Flame; Blaze; Brilliant
Jvalita	Flame; Blaze; Kindle
Jyo	Advise; Instruct; Vow; Order; Observe
Jyothi	Illumination; luminosity; effulgence
Jyoti	Light; Sun; Fire
Jyotihsvarupa	Form of light
Jyotika	Light; Flame
Jyotirmayi	Full of light
Jyotishmati	Full of light
Jyotsnā	Moon light; Light; Splendor; Brahma; Epithet of Durga

Jyotsnika	Moon light night
Tanmaya	Observed into god; Become one
Tanu	Graceful; Delicate
Tanu	Body; thin
Tanuja	Belong to body; Daughter
Tanyata	Roaring; Thunder; Wind
Tapana	Burning; Shining; Epithet of the Sun
Tapasvini	Ascetic; one who is practising Tapas
Tapati	River; Daughter of the Sun
Tara	Surpassing; Conquering; Overpowering; Excelling
Tara	Name of God as the Divine Mother
Tarani	Energetic; Benevolent; The Sun; Ray of light
Taranya	Passing over; Crossing over
Tarika	Belong to stars; Float; Boat
Taritā	Form of Goddess Durga
Tarpita	Gratified; Pleasing; Satisfied

Tāttvika	Accordant with reality; Real; True; Essential
Tautika	Pearl; Pearl Oyster
Tavya	Powerful; Strong
Tejasvi	Brilliant; Splendid; Bright; Powerful; Glorious; Noble
Tejasvini	Brilliant; Splendid; Bright; Powerful; Glorious; Noble
Tejasvini	Brilliancy; the element of fire
Tejasya	Splendid; Conspicuous
Tejita	Sharp; Witted; Polish; Invigorated
Tejomaya	Having splendor or light; Shining; Brilliance; Luminous; Glorious
Tejomayi	Full of light; resplendent
Titha	Fire; Love; Time; Autumn
Tosha	Satisfaction; Gratification; Contentment; Pleasure; Happiness
Toshana	Satisfaction; Gratification; Contentment; Pleasure; Epithet of Durga
Toshita	Satisfied; Pleased; Gratified; Appeased
Tripti	Satisfaction; Gratification; Contentment; Pleasure
Tripti	Satisfaction

Trishā	Strong desire; Wish
Trishna	Thirsting; internal craving
Trishnā	Strong Desire; Wish; Avidity
Turvani	Strong; Powerful; Excelling; Surpassing
Tusha	Rice; Grain; Corn
Tūshnika	Silent; Taciturn; Pure
Tushti	Satisfaction; Gratification; Contentment; Pleasure
Tuvi	Great; Strong; Powerful
Tvāshti	Name of goddess Durga
Tvāyā	Love towards Thee/Good; Love of Thee/God
Tvesha	Vehement; Impetuous; Inspiring awe; Brilliance; Bright; Glittering; Rudra
Tveshita	God's Gift; Sent by god
Tveshya	Shining; Brilliant; Epithet of Rudra
Tvishā	Light; Splendor; Ray; Brilliance; Beauty
Tvishi	Energy; Power; Splendor; Light; Ray; Brilliance; Beautiful; Rudra
Dādhrishi	Courageous; Bold; Overpowering

Daksha	Able; Competent; Expert; Brilliant; Intelligent; Upright; Honest
Daksha	Expert; intelligent; wise; able
Dakshatā	Cleverness; Ability; Efficiency
Dākshya	Cleverness; Dexterity; Skill; Ability; Integrity
Damayati	To subdue; Over-power; Conquer
Damita	Tamed; Subdued; Patient of suffering or exaction or privation
Darsha	Looking at; Viewing; Perceiving; Appearance; The Moon
Darshika	Spectator; Seeing; Examining; Displayed; Skillful
Darshita	Visible; Beautiful; Conspicuous; The Sun; The Moon
Darsini	Insight; way of seeing; vision; system of philosophy; making visible
Dasmya	Wonderful; Extraordinary; Beautiful
Dayita	Desired; Cherished; Beloved; Dear
Devayani	The path of the gods
Devika	Devine; Celestial; God-like
Deya	Gift; Given; Presented
Dhanya	Wealthy; Opulent; Fortunate; Happy; Best; Lucky; Auspicious; Virtuous

Dharani	The Earth; The Soil
Dharmishtha	Very Pious; Virtuous; Lawful; Righteousness
Dharni	Bearing; Supporting; Strong; Energetic; Powerful
Dhātri	Devine bearing who is creator, maintainer and manager; The Brahma
Dhavala	Dazzling; Shining White; White Color: Beautiful
Dhita	Pleased; Satisfied; Adorable; Lovable
Dhiti	Thought; Notion; Reflection; Idea; Understanding; Wisdom
Dhrishita	Bold; Courageous; Brave; Daring
Dhrishni	Ray of light
Dhritā	Held; Borne; Carried; Maintained; Supported
Dhriti	Holding; Steadiness; Steadfastness; Fortitude; Strong will
Dhriti	Patience and firmness
Dhruti	Destiny; Fate
Dhruvi	Firmly fixed; Firm
Dhyanika	Pertaining to Dhyana or meditation
Dhyati	Have in mid; Meditate; Imagine; Reflect upon

Didhiti	Splendor; Brightness; Light
Diksha	Initiation; consecration
Dipa	Light; Lamp
Dipaka	Kindling; Illuminating; Bright; Illustrating; Beautifying
Dipāli	Row of lights
Dipika	Kindling; Illuminating; Bright; Illustrating; Beautifying
Dipti	Brightness; Brilliancy; Splendor; Light; Beauty; Loveliness
Diti	Splendor; Bright; Shining
Diva	Heaven; Sky; Paradise; Day
Divya	Devine; Heavenly; Celestial; Light; Shine; Bright; Splendid
Divya	Divine; heavenly; celestial; sacred; luminous
Dridha	Firm; unshaken
Drishta	The visible; seen; that which is perceived
Drisya	Perceived; seen; the world; that which can be seen
Druti	Patience; Virtue
Duvanya	Worshipping

Duvasya	Honour; Worship; Celebrate; Acknowledge
Duvasyu	Honouring; Worshiping
Dyuksha	Heavenly; Celestial; Light; Brilliant; Epithet of Varuna, Agni, Indra
Dyumani	Jewel of Sky; The Sun; Epithet of Shiva
Dyuti	Splendor; Brightness; Brilliance; Light; Majesty; Dignity
Nabha	To bind; Connect; Connecting Heaven and Earth; Sky
Nabhanu	Spring; River
Nābhasa	Celestial; Heavenly; Appearing in the Sky
Nadaha	Lovely; Beautiful; Desirable
Nadya	Connected with a river
Nalini	Lotus flower; Water Lilly
Namasya	Worshipped; Adored; Venerable; Respectable; Reverential; Humble
Namita	Bowed; Bent down; Salutation; Obeisance
Namrata	Humility
Namratā	Bowed down; Venerable; Salutation; Obeisance
Namya	Bowed down; Venerable; The night

Nandikā	An epithet of Gauri
Navishti	Praise; Sacrifice; Oblation
Navya	Young; Fresh; Ever new; Praised; Laudable
Nayana	Leading; Guiding; Conducting; Managing
Nibha	Like; Resembling; Similar; Handsome-faced
Nidhi	Treasure-house of good qualities; Person with good qualities; Collection of Wealth, Valuables
Nidhruvi	Constant; Persevering; Faithful
Nidhyāna	Intuition; Looking at; Seeing at; Beholding; Sight
Nidhyāta	Meditated on; thought on; Imagination; Reflection
Nigama	Sacred; Words from God or holy man; Certainty; Assurance
Nigamana	Conclusion
Nihspriha	Desirelessness
Nihsreyas	Supreme Bliss; Moksha
Nimagna	Immersed in; Deeply involved; Fallen into; Submerged;
Nimesha	Twinkling of an eye; a moment or minute
Nimi	Fixed in; Dig in; Fix; Erect

Nimisha	Twinkling; Winking; Shutting the eye; Son of Garuda; Epithet of Vishnu
Ninīshu	Desirous to take or lead; Wishing to bring; Wishing to Spend time
Nirah	Express; Pronounce; Express
Nīraja	Free from Dust; Free from passion; Epithet of Shiva
Nirajana	Burning of camphor and the like; an offering or waving of camphor or any light before the deity during worship
Nirati	Delighted in; Attachment to
Nirmala	Spotless; Stainless; Clear; Clean; Pure
Nirmala	Without impurity; pure
Nirmoha	Without attachment; without delusion
Nirūdhi	Fame; Celebrity; Renown
Nirukta	Express; Pronounce; Express; Define; Explain
Nirupana	Investigation or ascertainment
Nisarga	Nature; Natural Creation; Natural Condition
Nishā	Night; Dream; Vision
Nishamya	Having seen; Having heard; Having tranquillized; Put out as light
Nishata	Candid; Honest; Genuine

Nishi	Sharp; Stimulate; Excite
Nishita	Sharped; Witted; Pointed; Stimulated
Nishītha	Night; The Moon
Nishiti	Excitement; Stimulation; Encouragement
Nishtha	Steadfastness; establishment in a certain state
Nishthā	Eminence; Excellence; Perfection; Intent to; Skilled in; Practicing in
Nisrita	Name of a river; Gone forth
Nīta	Lead; Guide; Conduct; Manage; Wealth
Nīti	Guidance; Directing; Managing; Propriety; Policy; Right, moral, Prudent Behavior
Nitya	Continual; Perpetual; Eternal; Everlasting; Invariable
Nitya	Eternal; daily; obligatory; permanent
Nityamukta	Eternally free
Nityasuddha	Eternally pure
Nityata	Eternity
Nivedita	Made Known; Announced; Reported; Communicated; Entrusted; Presented; Given

Niyata	Checked; Curbed; Restrained; Self-governed; Self-controlled; Attentive
Niyati	Restrain; Fixed order of things; Destiny; Fate; Luck; Self-command; Goddess Aayati
Niyu	Bestow; Harness; Join; Confer
Nritya	Dance; Lord Siva's Dance is known as the Tandava Nritya
Nriyagna	Service of human beings; one of the five daily sacrificial rites; feeding of the guest, the poor
Nyasa	Renunciation; laying down
Pānya	Praiseworthy; Excellent
Paramjyothi	Supreme Light; Brahman
Pari	Beyond; More than; In the way
Parichiti	Acquaintance; Familiarity
Paridā	Giving one's self to favour or protection of another; Surrender; Devotion
Parignā	Knowledge; Accurate; Ascertain
Parinī	To lead; To trace out; Discover; Investigate
Parinishthā	Perfect skill; Conversancy; Complete achievement
Parinishtita	Completely Skilled; Acquainted with

Pārshata	Epithet of Durgā
Pārshni	Divinity
Paurnima	An Ascetic; Day of full moon
Pavitra	Purified; Clean; Sacred
Praagna	A name according to Vedanta Philosophy of the individual in the causal state
Prabala	Strong; Powerful; Mighty; Great
Prabha	Light; Splendor; Radiance; Ray of light; Morning; Epithet of Durga
Prabhasana	Shining; Irradiating; Illuminating
Prada	Give away; Deliver; Present; Offer
Pradhi	Great Intelligence; Superior intelligence; Preeminently intelligent
Pradipti	Light; Lustre; Splendor; Brilliancy
Pragna	Wise; Intelligent; Learned
Pragnatha	Knowledge
Pragnhati	Knowing the way; Knowing the right way
Praharshita	Extremely delighted; Greatly delighted; Very happy
Prajvala	Kindle; Light; Fire; Blaze

Prakhya	Praise; Extol; Celebrate; Acknowledge
Prakul	Handsome; Excellent body
Prameya	Object of proof; subject of enquiry; object of right knowledge; measured or known object
Pramodita	Delighted; Rejoiced; Pleased; Happy
Pranati	Salutation; Reverence; Bending; Bowing; Inclination
Pranaya	Leading; Guiding; Confidence; Trust; Leader; Friendship; Kindness
Praneeti	Conduct; Leading; Guidance; favour
Pranshu	Great Stature; High; Tall; Lofty
Prapti	A power by which the Yoga gets everything; one of the eight major Siddhis
Prapurna	Fulfilling; Satisfying; Bow
Prarthana	Desire; Wish; Longing; Prayer; Entreaty; Request
Prasanna	Brightness; Clearness; Purity; Pleased; Delighted; Gracious
Prashanti	Becoming Calm; Tranquil; Calm; Quite; Pacification; Composure
Pratha	Fame; Celebrity; Spreading out
Pratham	First; Desiring; Epithet of Lord Ganesh; Foremost
Prathiksha	Look forward; Expect; Wait; Bear with; Tolerate

Prathiti	Celebrity; Notoriety
Pratibha	Brilliant; Intelligent; Understanding; Light; Genius
Pratika	Turned towards; Directed towards; Outward firm or shape
Pratika	An image or symbol of God for worship and spiritual contemplation
Pratima	Image; Idol; Likeness; Resembling; Creator; Maker; Framer
Pratima	A copy; an image made of any metal, wood or similar material for worship or spiritual contemplation
Pratishtha	Standing firmly; Strong; Famous; Foundation; Fixity
Pratistha	Reputation; fame; Rini resting; establishment; installation
Praveena	Skillful; Clever; Proficient; Conversant; Versed
Pravigna	Complete Knowledge; Know completely; Know accurately
Pravinya	Cleverness; Dexterity; Skillful; Proficiency; Accurate knowledge; Conversancy
Preeti	Pleasurable sensation; Pleasure; Joy; Gladness; Happiness; Enjoyment
Prekshaya	Looked at; To be regarded; Apparent; Brilliantly conspicuous; Worthy of seeing
Prekshita	Looked at; Viewed; Beheld; Seen; Glance
Prema	Love; Affection; Kind; Tender; Regard; Favour

Prishni	Earth; Cloud; Milk; The Spangled or starry sky; Ray of light
Prishti	Ray of light; Touch
Priya	Beloved; Dear; Valued; Amiable; Liked; Desired; Agreed
Priya	Bliss; joy derived on seeing a beloved object
Priyadarshani	Looking with kindness
Priyamvada	Speaking Kindly, Pleasantly, Agreeably; Sweet speaking
Priyodita	Well spoken; Kindly spoken; Pleasingly uttered
Puja	Worship; adoration
Pūja	Adore; Honour; Revere; Worship
Pūjita	Worshiped; Honoured; Reverence
Pūjya	To be Honoured; Respected; Adoration
Pulakita	Bristling up with Joy; Thrilled with joy; Delighted; Rejoiced; Enraptured
Puna	Purifying; Cleaning
Punya	Good; Pure; Holy; Right; Virtuous; Sacred; Auspicious
Punya	Merit; virtue
Purna	Full; complete; infinite; absolute; Brahman

Pushpa	Flower; Blossom; Gallantry; Politeness
Pushpita	Flowered; Blossom; Full of Flowers; Blooming
Pushya	Blossom; Nakshatra; Prince; Buddha
Pūtrima	Purified; Pure; Clean
Bhanu	Brightness; appearance; Light the Sun; Ray of light
Bhargavi	Epithet of Lakshmi; Epithet of Parvathi
Bhavana	Being; Existing; Becoming; Birth; Nature; Adobe; Dwelling
Bhavani	Goddess Parvathi
Bhavati	To serve for; Tend to conduce; To possess
Bhavika	Suitable; Prosperous; Happy; Welfare
Bhavita	To thrive; Protected; Cherished; Fostered; Transformation; Imagination
Bhogya	Enjoyable; Endured; Experienced; Useful; Profitable
Bhumi	The Earth; Soil; Ground; Position; Situation
Bhumika	Earth; Ground; Soil; Story; Flat; Custom; Decorating images; Character
Bhumika	Step or stage; state; degree
Bhuvah	The higher etheric or the astral world

Bhuvana	World
Bhuvani	Being; Living; World; Mankind; The heaven; The earth; Bring into existence
Bindu	Drop; Spherical; Point; Detached particle; Descendent of Agni
Bindu	Point; dot; seed; source; the basis from which emanated the first principle, Mahat-tattva
Maala	Rosary; beads used for Japa
Madhu	Pleasant Taste or flavour; Agreeable; Sweet; Nectar of flowers
Madhura	Sweet; Honey; Pleasant; Attractive; Melodious
Madhura	The attitude of a devotee expressing the emotion
Magha	Gift; Donation: Present; Reward; Wealth; Power
Māhātmika	High minded; Magnanimous; Noble; Majestic; Honored; Glorious
Māhesi	Goddess Durga
Mahi	Great; Large; Intellect
Mahima	Greatness; Magnitude; Grandeur; Majesty; Glory
Mahima	Glory; one of the eight major Siddhis
Mahina	Great; Powerful; Extensive
Mahira	The Sun

Mahita	Honoured; celebrated; Revered; Esteemed
Mahiya	To be glad; To be joyous; To be Happy; Raise to high position
Maitreyi	Friendly; Friend; Benevolent; Buddha
Maitri	Friendliness
Mālati	Jasmine flower; Blossom; Bud; Young woman; Moon shine; Night
Mālika	Related or belong to garland
Mālini	Garlanded; Crowned; Wearing necklace
Mamata	Mineness
Manasa	Word and thought; Goddess;
Manasya	Have in Mind; Intend; Think; Reflect
Mandira	Habitation; Adobe; Temple; Stable
Mangala	Happiness; Felicity; Good fortune; Good luck; Success; Prosperity; Bliss
Manisha	Thought; Reflection; intellect; Wisdom; Sagacity; Intelligence
Manisha	Independent power of thinking
Manita	Honoured; Respected
Manju	Beautiful; Lovely; Charming; Pleasing; Agreeable; Sweet

Manjula	Beautiful; Pleasing; Agreeable; Sweet; Soft
Manogna	Beautiful; Lovely; Charming; Pleasing; Agreeable; Sweet
Manolaya	Conquest of the mind
Manya	Respected; Honoured; Venerable
Mauna	Silence
Maunika	Resembling a Muni; Inspired Sage; Like Muni
Maya	Illusory; Possessing magical powers; Trick; Unreal
Maya	The illusive power of Brahma; the veiling and power of the universe
Medha	Power of retaining the import of studies
Megha	A Cloud; Multitude; Poet; Mountain; Name of Raga
Mihira	Cloud; Wind; Air; The Sun; The Moon
Modita	Pleased; Gratified; Delighted
Moha	Infatuation; delusion caused by wrong thinking
Mohana	Fascinating; Infatuated; Depriving of Consciousness or sensation
Mohini	Illusive; Fallacious; Alluring; Fascinating
Mohita	Illusion; Fascinating; Infatuated; Perplexed

Moksha	Emancipation; Deliverance; Freedom; Liberation
Moksha	Release; liberation; the term is particularly applied to the liberation
Mokshita	Set free; Let go; Liberated; Allowed to be large
Mridula	Soft; Tender; Mild; Gentle
Mrinalini	Lotus flower; Water Lilly
Mudita	Complacency; joy
Mugdha	Young; Beautiful; Lovely; Charming; Tender; Attractive
Mugdha	The state of very deluded forgetfulness of real divine nature
Mukti	Liberation; Deliverance; Freedom
Mukti	Release; liberation; the term is particularly applied to the liberation
Yakshati	Worship; Honour; Reverence
Yāmi	Personification of Yamuna river; Sister; Female relation
Yāmini	The Moon; Night
Yamuna	Celebrated River raises from Himalaya
Yāna	Way; Path; Road; Retreat; Journey; Procession
Yashasya	Famous; Glorious; Renowned; Celebrated; Honoured

Yoshita	Woman; Female
Yūnī	Young; youthful; Natural strength; Strong; Healthy; Agni
Rachana	Act of making; Formation; Creation; Literary production; Arrangement
Rachana	Creation; construction
Rachita	Made; Formed; Produced; Made ready; Composed; Written; Decorated
Rādhā	Beauty; Splendor; Light; Lustre
Raga	Blind love; attraction; attachment that binds the soul to the universe
Ragini	Passionate; Loving; Affectionate
Rajani	Goddess Durga; To colour; Night
Rajishta	Most Honest; Upright
Rajita	Highly delighted: Affected; Moved; Influenced
Rājni	Queen; Princess; Wife of King
Raksha	Guardian; Protector; Care; Preservation
Rakshita	Guarded; Protected; Taken care
Ram	Stay Calm; Tranquillize; Happy; Rejoice; Please

Ramani	Pleasing; Gratifying; Delighting; Rejoicing
Rāmila	Lover; Love of god
Ramya	Enjoyable; Pleasing; Delightful; Agreeable
Ranjita	Highly delighted: Affected; Moved; Influenced
Rasasvada	Tasting the essence or the bliss of Savikalpa Samadhi
Rashmi	Ray of light; Beam; Shine
Rashmika	Shining; Ray of Light
Rasika	Graceful; Passionate; Elegant; Beautiful
Ratna	Gift; Present; Property; Riches; Possessions
Ratna	Gem; jewel; the best
Ratū	River of heaven; The Celestial Ganges; A true speech
Renu	Pollen of flowers; Sand particles
Ridhma	Love; Spring
Rishika	A Sage; A Princess; Name of a river
Rita	True; correct; real
Ritvika	Priest performing a sacrifice

Rocha	Lightening; Illuminating; One who lightens or makes bright
Rochana	Enlightening; Making bright; Splendid; Beautiful
Roha	Raising; Mounting; Growing; Bud; Blossom
Rohi	Kind of Deer; Seed; Tree; Observing a vow; Religious
Rohini	A Star; A cow; Raising; Mounting up; Growing; Long; Tall
Ruchi	Light; Lustre; Appetite; Wish; Desire; Inclination; Taste for
Ruchi	Taste; appetite; liking; desire
Rudrāni	Goddess Durga
Ruha	Rising; Mounting; Growing on; Producing on
Ruhāna	Attaining; Gaining; Delighting
Rukmini	Wearing golden ornaments; Decorated with gold
Ruksha	Shining; Brilliant; Radiant; Glittering
Rupa	Appearance; form; sight; vision
Lalita	Lovely; Beautiful; Handsome; Elegant; Graceful
Lashita	Wished; Desired
Lāsya	Dance; Dancing; Female dancer; Singing; Dance with emotion of love

Latā	Creeping plant; String of pearls; Slender or Graceful women
Latikā	Small creeping plant; String of pearls
Lāvanya	Beauty; Loveliness; Charming
Laya	The act of Clinging; Adhering; Sticking; Embrace; Fusion
Laya	Dissolution; merging
Laya chintana	Concentration of the mind with a view to dissolve it; kind of Vedantic meditation
Lekha	Writing; Letter; Epistle; Manuscript; A god; Deity
Likhita	Scratched; Scraped; Sacrificed; Written
Lila	Play; sport; the cosmos looked upon as a divine play
Lilamayi	A connotative name of the divine force
Lina	Dissolved; merged; lost
Lipsā	Desired to gain; Wish to acquire or obtain; Desire of possessing
Lipsitā	To be wished; To be obtain; To be acquired; Desired
Lipsya	To be wished; To be obtain; To be acquired; Eligible
Lochana	Illuminating; Brightening; Visible; Buddhist Goddess
Urvasi	Wish; Desire

Usha	Shine; Brilliant; Morning light
Vāgdevi	Goddess of Speech or eloquence
Vaishnavi	Personified shakti of Vishnu; Goddess Durga
Vaishnavi	The Sakti or the divine power of Vishnu
Vanamala	The picturesque garland worn by Lord Vishnu
Vandana	Praise; Worship; Adoration; Reverence; Worship; Obeisance
Vandya	Praiseworthy; Laudable; Commendable; Honoured; worshiped
Vanita	Wished; Desired; Loved; Served
Vanusha	To obtain; Acquire; To worship
Vanushya	To wish for; To desire
Varishtha	Most Excellent; Best; Dearest; Most Preferable; Greatest
Varsha	Rain; Rainy season; A cloud; A year
Varshika	Raining; Rainy; Shedding; Showering; Pouring down
Varshini	Rain; Raining; Showering; Sprinkling
Varshita	Rain; Raining
Vasantha	To shine; Spring season

Vāsavi	Belong to Indra; Name of Indra
Vashya	Humble; Obedient; Dutiful; Docile
Vasvi	Glorious; Excellent
Veda	True knowledge; Devine knowledge
Veni	Loving; Desiring
Vibhā	Light; Lustre; Ray of light; Beauty
Vibhāva	Shining; Splendid; Epithet of Sunrise
Vibhavya	Distinguishable; To be clearly perceived; Observed; Remarkable
Vibushit	Adorn; Decorated; Ornamented
Vigna	Distinguish; Right Knowledge; Intelligent; Wise; Learned
Vihasana	Laugh gently; Smile
Vihasita	Laugh gently; Smile
Vihasya	Laugh gently; Smile
Vihiti	Action; Performance; Doing; Arranging
Vijaya	Conquest; Victorious; Overcome; Overpower; Win
Vijiti	Conquest; Victory; Triumph over; vanquishing

Vikānkshā	Freedom from desire or eagerness, hesitation
Vikranti	Stepping on; Striding; Heroism; Velour; Power; Prowess
Viksha	Sight; Gazing; Seeing; Surprise; Astonishment
Vikshana	Act of seeing; Looking at; Observing; Sight
Vikshaya	Visible; Perceptible; Observable
Vikshita	Seen; Viewed; Beheld; Regarded; Considered
Vikshita	A look; To look; Perceive
Vilāsana	Merriness; Pastime; Play; Dalliness; Grace; Elegance; Charm; Beauty
Vilohita	An epithet of Rudra; Fire; Deep red or purple colour
Vilokya	Having looked at; Having seen, observed, perceived, witnessed; Regard; Attention
Vindu	Intelligent; Knowing; Liberal; Munificent; Detached particle; Bindu
Vinīta	Well trained; Well educated; Disciplined; Modest; Virtuous
Vinīti	Training; Good behavior; Reverence; Obeisance
Vinodini	Pleasure; Enjoyment; Gratification; Eagerness; Vehemence
Vinodita	Delighted; Happy; Allayed; Soothed
Vipula	Abundant; Deep; Profound; Plenty; The Earth

Virochana	Shining; Illuminating; The Sun; The moon; The fire
Vishah	Endure; Bear; Sustain; Determine; Conquer
Vishārada	Learned; Wise; Skillful; Conversant with; Famous; Celebrated
Vishok	Free from sorrow; Happy
Vishruti	Fame; Celebrity; Notoriety
Vishvi	Shine forth; Manifest; Spread or extend in all directions
Visinī	Lotus flowers; Assemblage of Lotus flowers
Vivardhita	Increased; Gratified; Advanced; Delighted
Vivechana	Act of discrimination (Truth from falsehood, reality from semblance); Judgement
Vivechita	Discriminated (Truth from falsehood, reality from semblance); Distinguished
Vivriti	Expansion; Manifestation; Interpretation; Discovery
Vrinda	Numerous; Name of the forest in which Krishna was educated; Tulasi
Vrishini	Having fond of rain; Peacock
Vrishti	Rain; A shower
Sachana	Act of honouring, favouring, assisting; Honour; Service

Sachetana	Possessed of consciousness
Sadā	Always; At all times; Continually; Perpetually; Ever
Sadriksha	Like; Resembling; Similar look
Sadrishi	Like; Resembling; Same; Similar look
Sahana	Patience; Endurance; Forbearance
Sahasya	Related to strength; Strong; Vigorous
Sahita	Accompanied or attended by; Associated or connected with
Sahya	Powerful; Sweet; Agreeable; Endured
Sakshi	Witnessing principle; seer; witness
Sākshi	Witness; Evidence; Testimony; Attestation
Sakshi chaitanya	Witnessing intelligence or consciousness
Sakshi chetana	Witnessing soul; witnessing intelligence or consciousness
Samāgnā	Reputation; Fame
Samantha	Quite; Tranquility; Calmness of mind; Absence of passion
Samanvita	Connected; Associated with; Fully endowed; Possessed by
Samarchana	The act of honouring, worshiping, adoration

Samarchita	Honoured; Worshiped; Adored
Samata	Balanced state of mind
Samharshini	Possessing Joy; Delight; Unruptured
Samhita	Put together; Placed together; Combined; united; Endowed; Provided
Samhita	Collection; one of the two primary sections of each of the Vedas
Samhrishta	Thrilled; enraptured; Rejoiced; Delighted; Glad
Samīhā	Striving after; Long for; Desire for
Samīhita	Longed or wished for; Desired; Undertaken
Samikshita	Well looked at; Perceived, considered; To be investigated
Samīkshita	To behold; Perceive; Consider; Mind
Samira	Cause to move; Excited; Revive; Confer; Bestow; Wind; Air
Samīshita	Extended; Stretched out; Lengthened
Samistha	Sacrificed together; Sacrificed
Samīya	Similar; To be treated with equally or in the same manner
Samprayoga	Contact of the senses with the objects
Sampriti	Attachment; Affection; Friendly assent; Delight

Samshita	Accomplished; Established; Determined; Well ascertained
Samshraya	Seeking alliance; Mutual protection; Patronage; Name of Prajapati
Samshrita	Seek protection; Sheltered; Secured; Protected; Supported
Samsmrita	Remembered; Recollected; Called to mind
Samsrishti	Mingled; Mixed together; Connected; United; Composed
Samudvi	To look at; To perceive
Samvi	To perceive
Samvita	Knowledge; consciousness; intelligence
Samyama	Perfect restraint; balanced repose, concentration, meditation
Samyojya	Joined together; United; Having enjoined or directed
Samyukta	Conjoined; Joined with; Connected; Attached; Mixed; Accompanied
Samyukta	United; combined
Sanā	Always; Eternally; Perpetually
Sanāya	Act like an immortal being; Be eternal
Sanchali	Move about; pass through; Quivering
Sanchita	Collection; Accumulate; Gather; Save

Sandhyā	Joining together; Twilight; Evening; Twilight personified as daughter of Brahma
Sandrishti	Compete sight; Full view; A sight; Glance; Look; Aspect
Sangīta	Singing together; Sing in harmony or chorus
Sangīti	Singing together; Concert; Symphony; Harmony;
Sangna	Agree together; Mutual understanding; Live in harmony
Sangnata	Known; Understood; Destined or intended for
Sanishtha	Most liberal or bountiful; Very munificent
Sanishya	To wish to give; To wish for; To desire for gifts
Sanjana	Bright forth; Generate; Produce; To cause to be born; Create; Epithet of Brahma, Shiva
Sanjayanti	Conquering; Victorious
Sanjiti	Complete victory
Sanjīvini	Rendering alive; Enlivening; Restoring life
Sankalpa	Thought, desire; imagination
Sankīrtana	The act of reciting or proclaiming at full; Greatly praising or celebrating
Sankshipti	Abridgement; Brevity; Throwing; Sending; Transition

Santoshi	Satisfaction; Contentedness; Happiness; Delight; Joy; Pleasure
Sāra	Essence; The substantial or essential part of anything; Strength; Power; Vigour
Sarupya	Having the same form as God
Sarvagna	Omniscient; knowing everything
Sarvānī	Name of Drug; Wife of lord Shiva
Sasya	Good quality; Excellent; Merit
Sāttvika	Name of goddess Durga; Worshiper of Durga
Satya	True; Real; Genuine; Sincere; Honest; Virtuous
Saujanya	Goodness; Generosity; Kindness; Compassion; Benevolence; Friendship
Saumya	The Moon; Handsome; Pleasing; Gentle; Soft
Shachi	Speech; Powerful speech; Eloquence; Diligence; Energy
Shakti	Ability; Power; Capacity; Faculty; Strength; Energy
Shama	Tranquility; Rest; Calm; Peace
Shāmbhavi	Belong to Shiva; Worshipper of Siva; Goddess Parvati
Shamikā	Pacifying; Tranquilizing; Consolatory
Shamini	Calm; Tranquil; Appeased; Pacified

Shamita	Appeased; Pacified; Calmed; Relaxed
Shamyā	Knowledge; Understanding
Shankari	Wife of lord Shiva
Shansya	Praised; Praiseworthy; Meritorious; To be wished; Desirable
Shanta	Calm; Pacified; Quite; Tranquil
Shanti	Be calm; Peace; Rest; Tranquility, Bliss
Shāradha	Name of Saraswathi; Goddess Durga
Sharala	Upright; Honest; Pure minded
Sharani	Road; Path; Way; The Earth
Sharanya	To be protected; Name of Durga; Epithet of Shiva
Sharayū	Name of the river
Shardha	Strength; Power; Multitude; Breaking wind
Sharmishtā	Most fortunate
Sharvānī	Goddess Parvati; Wife of lord Shiva
Sharyanā	Sweet as honey; Name of the lake
Shashthi	Sixth day of lunar foresight; Epithet of Durga

Shasya	Praised; Praiseworthy; Meritorious; To be wished; Desirable; Excellent; Best
Sheela	Disposition; Inclination; Character; Nature; Tendency; Behaviour; Conduct
Sheetal	Cool; Cold; Frigid; Chilly; Cool breezes; The Moon
Shikhā	Sharp end; Highest point; Peak; Pinnacle; Summit; Ray of light
Shilpa	An art; Any manual or mechanical or fine art; Architecture; Enumerated
Shimi	Power; Strength; Energy
Shivāni	Wife of lord Shiva
Shobha	Light; Lustre; Radiance; Splendor; Brilliancy; Beauty
Shobhana	Adorning; Causing to look beautiful; Shining; Splendid; Auspicious; Virtuous
Shobita	Beautiful; Adorned; Decorated; Splendid
Shochistha	Shining very much; Most brilliant
Shodhitā	Cleansed; Purified; Pure; Clean
Shraddhā	To place confidence in; Have faith, trust, belief
Shravasya	To desire fame or glory; To desire a sacrifice or oblation; Praiseworthy; Celebrated
Shrāvya	Worthy of being listen to; To be heard

Shrīla	Fortune; Prosperous; Rich; Wealthy; Famous; Celebrated
Shriyā	Fortune; Happiness; Prosperity; Wife of Vishnu
Shruti	Audition; Hearing; Oral account; Report; Intelligence; Revelation
Shubham	Bright; Shining; Splendid; Beautiful; Fortunate; Happy; Virtuous; Eminent
Shuchi	Bright; Clever; Clean; Cleansed; Purified; Virtuous; Holy; Pious; Honest
Shuchita	Cleansed; Purified; Pure; Clean
Shuchiya	To become pure or white; To be holy
Shushma	Very Strong; Powerful; Vigour; The Sun; Prowess; Light; Lustre
Shushrusha	Desire or wish to hear; Desire to obey; Obedience; Service
Shveta	White; White colour; Dressed in white; A mountain range
Shvetauhi	Wife of Indra
Sima	All; Every; Whole; Entire
Sindhu	The Ocean; Sea; Name of a River
Sloka	Verse of praise; a verse generally consisting of 32 letters
Slokha	Praise; Hymning in verse; Celebrity; Renown; Fame; Reputation
Smarana	Remembrance

Smarta	Pertaining to or enjoined by the Smriti
Smrita	Remembrance; Memory; Reminiscence; Calling to mind
Smriti	Remembrance; Memory; Reminiscence; Calling to mind
Smriti	Memory; code of law
Sneha	Adhesiveness; friendship
Sphurana	Throbbing or breaking; bursting forth; vibration
Spriha	Desire; hankering
Sraddha	Faith
Sri	Goddess Lakshmi; wealth; prosperity
Srishti	Creation
Sruti	The Vedas; the revealed scriptures heard; ear
Sucharita	Good conduct; Well conducted; Well behaved; Faithful
Sudhā	Well-being; Welfare; Happiness; Ease; Comfort; Nectar; Honey
Sukhyāti	Good report; Fame; Celebrity
Sukrita	Good act; merit
Sukriti	Doing well; Acting in friendly or kind manner; Virtuous; Religious

Surabhi	Sweet smelling; Agreeable; Charming; Pleasing; Handsome; Famous; Wise; Virtuous
Susila	One whose nature is purified
Susmita	Pleasantly smiling; Women with pleasing or smiling countenance
Suvarchala	Wife of the Sun; Wife of Rudra
Suyukta	Well joined; Harmoniously combined; Epithet of Shiva
Svādhi	Well minded; Thoughtful; Contemplative; Meditating
Svadhita	Well read; Well versed in or conversant with
Svanika	Having beautiful lustre; Very radiant; Agni
Haima	Golden; Made of gold; Epithet of Shiva
Hansa	Swan; The vehicle of Brahma; Supreme Soul or universal spirit
Hansika	Female swan
Harini	Green; Green colour; Kind of grass; A Lion; Grass
Harita	Green; Green colour; Kind of grass; A Lion; Grass
Harshini	Rejoicing; Delighting
Harshita	Made glad and happy; Gladdened; Delighted
Haryanti	Desiring; Liking; Loving

Haryata	Beloved; Amiable; Agreeable; pleasant
Hāsini	Laughing; Smiling; Making merry
Hima	Cold season; Cold; The Moon; The Himalaya mountains
Himāni	Great frost; Mass of snow; Collection of Ice and snow
Hira	A diamond; A necklace; A thunderbolt; A lion; Name of Shiva

PART 2: BABY BOY NAMES

Abhi	Nearest; Dear
Abhijay	Conquest; Complete victory
Abhijit	Victorious; Born under constellation Abhijit; Name of Vishnu
Abhik	Affectionate
Abhikānksh	Long for; Desire; Strive for
Abhilāsh	Desire; Wish; Covetousness; Affection; Love
Abhinand	Rejoicing; Delighting; Applauding; Wish; Desire

Abhinandan	Rejoicing; Delighting; Applauding; Wish; Desire
Abhinav	Quite new; Young; Fresh; Having no experience
Abhinay	Controlling; training; disciplining
Abhinit	Brought near; Performed; Highly finished or ornamented; Fit, proper, kind, patient
Abhinivesh	Perseverance; Resolved; Inclination: Tenacity
Abhinivesh	Clinging to earthly life; will to live
Abhipsit	Desired; Wished
Abhir	Fearlessness; Undaunted; Terrific; Name of Bhairava or Shiva
Abhirām	Pleasing; Delightful; Agreeable; Beautiful; Epithet of Shiva
Abhirūpak	Corresponding; Pleasing, Handsome; Learned
Abhish	To seek for; To long for; Endeavour to gain
Abhishek	Sprinkling; Anointing; Inaugurating; Consecrating; Ablution; Worship
Abhrit	Clouded; Covered with clouds
Abjaja	An epithet of Brahma
Achal	Immovable; Mountain or rock; The Earth; Name of Lord Shiva
Achal	Not moving; fixed

Achyut	Imperishable; Not fallen; Firm; Name of Krishna, Vishnu
Achyut	Imperishable; Not fallen
Achyut	The indestructible; the unchanging
Adarsh	Ideal
Adhi	Master; Superior
Adhij	Born; Superior by birth
Adhiksh	Discover
Adhikshit	A Lord; Ruler; King
Adhip	Ruler; King; Sovereign
Adhish	Master; Lord; King
Adhit	Well read; Learned; Attained; Studied
Adhitya	Having gone over; Having studied
Adhokshaj	A being who cannot be perceived by the outer senses; a name of Bhagavan Narayana
Aditya	Sun-god; Sun; a class of celestial beings
Advait	Non-duality; monism
Advay	Unique; Only; Without second; Name of Buddha; Ultimate truth

Advesh	Not malevolent; Without opposition; Not to be disliked
Advitiy	Without a second
Agam	The Veda; manual of practical worship; profound
Agastiya	An epithet of lord Shiva
Agat	Stability
Agira	The Sun
Agni	Fire
Agnistut	He who sings the praises of Agni (in Vedic sacrifice)
Aharpati	The Sun
Ahin	Sacrifice
Ahuti	Oblation (poured into the fire in sacrifices)
Aindav	Related to the Moon; Lunar
Aindhan	An epithet of the Sun
Ajay	Unconquered; Unsurpassed; Invincible; Name of Lord Vishnu
Ajirshu	Ruler; Desirer
Ajit	Unconquered; Unsurpassed; Invincible; Irresistible; Name of Lord Vishnu, Shiva

Ajit	Invincible
Akhil	Complete; Whole; Without a gap
Akranti	Progress; Ascending
Aksh	The soul; Knowledge; Religious Knowledge; Law; Name of Garuda
Akshat	Unbroken; Whole; Name of lord Shiva
Akshay	Un-decaying; Imperishableness
Akshay	Un-decaying
Akshit	Undecayed; Uninjured; Un-decaying; Epithet of Indra
Alarka	Fabulous; Prince
Amama	Without selfishness or attachment or desire; Jaina saint
Amār	Immortal; Not dying
Amartya	Immortal
Ambikeya	An epithet of lord Ganesh
Amish	Luxury; Object of enjoyment, flesh
Amish	Honesty; Simplicity
Amit	Boundless; Infinite; Unmeasured

Amit	Infinite; Boundless
Amūdh	Not Infatuated; Not perplexed; Wise
Anagh	Innocent; Sinless; Faultless; Handsome; Epithet of Shiva
Anant	Endless; Boundless; Infinite; Epithet of Vishnu
Ananyata	Single-mindedness
Anchit	Reverenced; Honoured; Distinguished; Handsome; Curved
Anil	Air or wind in the deity form; Name of Rishi
Animish	Absence of winking; Vigilantly; Incessantly; Related to Gods
Aniruddha	Unobstructed; Ungoverned; Self-willed; Epithet of Shiva
Anish	Uninterrupted; Incessant; Night less; Related to God
Anji	Blessing
Anjishnu	Highly brilliant; The Sun
Anjishth	Highly brilliant; The Sun
Ankit	Marked; Numbered; Counted; Calculated
Ansh	Part; Portion; Inheritance; Earnest money; Name of Aditya
Anshul	Radiant; Name of Sage

Anunīt	Trained; Disciplined; Acquired; Respected; Humbly entreated; Pleased
Anūp	To preserve; To keep
Anupam	Incomparable; Matchless; Excellent; Best
Anurāg	Affection; Attachment; Love; Passion; Good will
Anurūp	Natural; Innate
Anvarth	Having the meaning; Obvious; Intelligible; Clear
Anvidh	To kindle
Anviksh	To follow with one's looks; Keep looking or gazing; To keep in view
Anvish	To desire; Seek; Seek after; Search; Aim at
Anvit	Joined; Connected; Essential or inherent part; Endowed; Possessed; Understood
Anvridh	Accomplish; To carry out
Apamanyu	Free from grief
Aparajit	Unconquerable
Apesh	To strive after; Aspire to
Apramey	Immeasurable

Apurv	Unseen; strange; extraordinary; the hidden power
Ara	Swift; Speedy; Jaina saint; Name of Ocean in Brahma's world
Aravind	Lotus flower
Arhan	Respect; Adoration; Worship
Arhant	Worthy; A Buddha; Name of Shiva
Arindam	Victorious; Conquering; Conqueror of enemies
Arjav	Simplicity; straightforwardness; rectitude conduct; uprightness
Arnav	The ocean of air; A wave, flood, stream
Arya	True; Devoted; Dear; Kind; Excellent; Noble
Ashok	Free from sorrow
Ashvin	A Star; Deity
Asmi	I am; I exist
Atarva	An epithet of lord Shiva; Piercy
Atharva	Name of Brahma's eldest son, to whom he revealed the Brahma-vidyā
Atharvana	Name of Shiva
Atmasray	Dependent on the Self for existence, as the case of Isvara

Atmavit	Knower of the Self
Atop	Pride
Atul	Unequalled; Surpassing
Avijnat	Unknown; Brahma
Avinash	Indestructible
Avyath	Fearlessness
Ayan	Road; Path; Going; Course; Period; Final emancipation
Ayan	Movement; the sun's passage
Ayut	Undisturbed; Inseparable
īkshan	Sight; Care; Superintendence
Isa	Lord
Ish	Search; A messenger
Ishān	Owning; Possessing; Wealthy; Reigning; Ruler; The Sun as son of Shiva
Ishir	Vigorous; Active; Refresh
Ishu	God of love
Iyant	Abundance; So much

Uday	Rise of Sun; Ascend; Prosperity
Uddav	Learned Disciple; Sacrificial fire
Unpendra	Lord Krishna; Lord Vishnu
Upen	Force; Strength; Drive
Urjit	Powerful; Strong; Mighty; Excellence
Utkarsha	Superiority; eminence
Uttam	The best; The great
Uttama	Best
Ojas	Vigour; spiritual energy; vitality; the spiritual force
Om	The Pranava or the sacred syllable
Omkar	The Pranava or the sacred syllable
Kaala	Time; death or Yama
Kailash	Paradise of Shiva; Mountain in Himalaya; Epithet of Shiva or Kubera
Kalki	Lord Vishnu 10th incarnation
Kalyan	Beautiful, Agreeable, Friendly, Noble
Kalyan	Auspicious; blessed

Kamal	Desire, Lotus, Goddess Lakshmi, Lord Brahma
Karunya	Compassion; Tenderness; Kindness
Kasi	The Sun; Handful
Kasyap	The Earth; Turtle; Sage
Kaunteya	Name of Arjuna
Kausik	Love; Passion; Epithet of Indra; Epithet of Shiva
Kedār	Mountain; Meadow
Kesa	Hair of the head; Epithet of Lord Vishnu
Kesari	Lion; Horse
Kesav	Lord Krishna; Lord Vishnu
Ketan	Invitation; Adobe; Symbol of Goddess
Keyur	An ornament worn on the arm of Lord Vishnu
Kirita	A crown; one of the ornaments of Lord Vishnu
Kodand	Bow; Eyebrow (shaped like bow)
Kovid	Leaned; Expert; Skillful; Wise
Kritin	Expert; Clever; Virtuous; Pure; Pious

Krittikeya	God of war
Kunāl	Lotus; Bird with beautiful eyes; A son of king Ashoka
Kundar	Epithet of Lord Vishnu
Kurma	Lord Vishnu, Turtle
Gadadhar	Wielder of the Gada; an epithet of Lord Vishnu
Gagan	Sky; Atmosphere; Heaven
Gagan	Sky; firmament
Gaganaravind	Sky-lotus; unreal or non-existent thing; the world
Gaira	Mountain; Mountaineer
Gambhir	Deep; magnanimous; dignified; grand; imperious; grave
Ganapati	Lord Ganesha; success-bestowing aspect of God
Gandiv	Bow of Arjuna
Gandivi	Name of Arjuna
Gaurav	Teacher; Guru; Honor; Esteem
Gautam	Name of the Buddha
Gayatri	One of the most sacred Vedic Mantras or texts of the Hindus

Ghora	Terrific; Frightful; Epithet of Shiva
Ghrish	Joyful; Lively; Happy; Merry
Giri	Hill; Mountain
Girikshit	Lord Vishnu
Gnanakar	Form of wisdom; Brahman; sage
Gnanamay	Full of knowledge
Guna	Quality born of nature
Gunamay	Full of qualities or attributes
Gunasamya	A state where the three Gunas are found in equilibrium; the Supreme Absolute
Gunavad	A statement of quality
Guru	Teacher; preceptor
Chaitanya	Intelligence; Mental Perception; Consciousness; Soul; Spirit
Chaitanya	The consciousness that knows itself an knows others; absolute consciousness
Chandānsu	The Sun; Hot rays
Chandila	Name of Rudra
Chandra	Moon; Light; Shining

Chandu	Pleasing; Lovely
Chang	Handsome; Beautiful; Dexterous; Clever; Healthy
Charan	Foot; one-fourth; conduct
Chidanand	Consciousness-Bliss
Chinmay	Intelligence; Thought; Mind; Soul
Chinmay	Full of Consciousness
Chiranjiva	Long lived; Epithet of Kama-deva
Chiranjivi	One who has gained deathlessness
Jagadguru	World preceptor
Jaishnav	Conqueror; Arjuna
Jaitra	Victorious; Triumphant
Jay	Victory; mastery
Jayant	Son of Indra; Epithet of Shiva; Rudra
Jina	Victorious; Triumphant
Jishnu	Victorious; Triumphant; Epithet of Indra, Vishnu, Arjuna
Jitamanyu	One who subdued his wrath; Epithet of Vishnu

Jitāri	Triumphant over enemy; a Buddha
Jitendra	One who has controlled the Indriyas or the senses
Jyotihsvarup	Form of light
Jyotirmay	Full of light
Jyotishmat	Full of light
Tanuvasin	Having power over the body; Epithet of Agni
Tapan	Burning; Desire
Tapas	Purificatory action; ascetic self-denial; austerity; penance
Tapasvi	Ascetic; one who is practising Tapas
Tarat	Passing over; Crossing over
Tarpan	Satisfying; Satiating; Pleasing; Refreshing
Tarun	Young; Tender; Juvenile; Lively; Vivid
Tej	Sharpness; Brilliancy; Spirit
Teja	Sharpness; Brilliancy; Spirit
Tejas	Sharpness; Sharp edge; Fierce; Top of the flame or ray; Brilliance; Fire
Tejas	Brilliancy; the element of fire

Tejasvi	Brilliancy; the element of fire
Tejomay	Full of light; resplendent
Toshak	Satisfaction; Gratification; Contentment; Pleasure; Happiness
Toshin	Satisfied; Contented; Pleased; liking; Gladdening
Trai	Protect; Preserve; Cherish; Defend
Trish	Strong desire; Thirsty; Long for; Wish
Trishu	Strong Desire; Moving Quickly; Rushing Violently
Tuhina	Snow; Cold; Frosty; Moonlight; Moonshine
Tunga	Elevated; Prominent; Erect; Chief; Strong
Tura	Strong; Powerful; Excelling; Surpassing
Turvan	Conquering; Defeating; Injuring enemy
Turyvā	Over powering; Superior Strength
Tushār	Snow; Cold; Frosty; Dowy
Tvakshyas	Efficiency; Energy; Vigor; Foe-destroying might
Tvāyat	Seeking Thee/God; Loving Thee/God
Tveshas	Force; Energy; Impulse; Brilliant energy

Tvish	Shining; Brilliance
Dālmi	Name of Indra
Dam	Tame; Subdue; Conquer; Tranquillized; Control; Restrain
Daman	Taming; Subduing; Over-powering
Damathu	Self-restrain; Self Subjugation; Self Control
Dansu	Wonderful Strength; Marvelous Deeds; Epithet of Indra
Dānu	Valiant; Victor; Conqueror; Shining; Brilliant
Darsan	Insight; way of seeing; vision; system of philosophy; making visible
Darshan	Showing the way; Leading; Exhibiting; Teaching; Epithet of Durga
Dāruk	Krishna's Charioteer; Incarnation of Lord Shiva
Dasa	Servant
Dashāmay	An epithet of Shiva
Dasya	The attitude of a devotee expressing the relationship of a servant with God
Datta	Given; Granted; Presented; Preserved; Guarded; Protected
Datta	Given; adopted; give.
Dāvan	Giving; Granting; Present

Daya	Mercy; compassion
Dayā	Taking interest in; Sympathy; Compassion; Mercy; Love; Clemency
Dāya	Gift; Donation: Present
Deva	Devine; Celestial; Heavenly
Devayan	The path of the gods
Devesh	Chief of gods; Epithet of Brahma, Vishnu, Shiva, Indra
Dhama	The Moon; Epithet of Krishna, Brahma; Supreme spirit
Dharan	Concentration of mind
Dharma	Righteous way of living; characteristics; virtue
Dhaval	Dazzling; Shining White; White Color: Beautiful
Dhira	Steadfast; bold; courageous
Dhīra	Determined; Resolved; Courageous; Strong; Brave; Daring
Dhirya	Intelligent; Wise; Clever; Prudent
Dhish	Praise, Celebrate
Dhrish	Courageous; Bold; Overpowering; Confident
Dhrishnu	Courageous; Bold; Confident; Valiant; Strong; Powerful

Dhrishu	Bold; Proud; Clever
Dhrit	A holder; Bearer; Possessor; Observing
Dhruva	Fixed; Firm; Stable; Enduring; Constant; Permanent; Strong
Dhyan	Meditation; contemplation
Dhyey	Object of meditation or worship; purpose behind action
Digambar	Naked; clad with the quarters
Digvijay	Conquest of the quarters (world), either military or cultural
Dikshit	Initiation; consecration
Dina	Humble; helpless
Dinadayal	Merciful towards the helpless
Dipankar	The Light maker; The Buddha
Dishnu	Giving; One who gives; A giver; Donor
Drughan	An epithet of Brahma
Druhan	An epithet of Shiva; Epithet of Brahma
Druhin	An epithet of Shiva; Epithet of Brahma
Dūta	Messenger; Carrier of Intelligence; Envoy; Ambassador

Duvas	Worship; Honour; Reverence; Wealth
Dyu	Agni; Fire; Brightness; Heaven; Sky
Dyujay	Conqueror of Heaven; Attainment of Heaven
Dyumna	Splendor; Glory; Majesty; Energy; strength; Power; Wealth; Inspiration
Dyut	Shining; Splendor; Ray of light; Bright; Brilliant
Nakshat	Strike down any one that approaches; Epithet of Indra
Nāmi	An epithet of Vishnu
Nanda	Happiness; Pleasure; Joy; Felicity; Prosperity
Nandan	Delight; Rejoice; Gladdening; Pleasing
Nandi	The Happy one; Epithet of Shiva
Nāndi	Joy; Satisfaction; Prosperity; Opening ceremony; Praise
Nandya	To be glad; To rejoice
Nigam	Sacred; Words from God or holy man; Certainty; Assurance
Nigam	Conclusion
Nikhil	Complete; All; Entire; Totally
Ninīshā	Wish to bring; Desire; Intention; Carrying; Leading

Nipun	Skilled; Expert; Clever; Adroit; Experience; Friendly
Nirajan	Burning of camphor and the like; an offering or waving of camphor or any light before the deity during worship
Nirmal	Spotless; Stainless; Clear; Clean; Pure
Nirmal	Without impurity; pure
Niruddha	Controlled
Nirukta	Etymology of the Vedas
Nirvana	Liberation; Eternal bliss; Emancipation
Nischay	Conviction; determination
Nishant	Tranquillized; Calm; Quite
Nishnāth	Well versed; Highly skilled; Clever; Learned; Superior
Nūtan	New; Novel; Recent; Modern; Fresh; Young
Parāg	Sandal; Fame; Celebrity; Independence
Paramesthi	The exalted one; a name generally applied It, Brahma
Paramjyothi	Supreme Light; Brahman
Parasamvit	Supreme knowledge or consciousness
Parikshit	Spreading around; Extend; Epithet of Agni

Pārindra	Lion
Parivid	Know thoroughly; Understand thoroughly
Pārtha	Prince; King; Epithet of Arjuna; Epithet of five sons of Pandu
Pava	Purity; Purification; Air; Wind
Pāvan	Purifier; Wind; Clean; Pure
Pavat	Purifying; Pure
Pāyu	Protector; Guard
Pinaka	The bow of Lord Siva
Pināka	Trident of Shiva
Piyūsh	Ambrosia; Nectar; Milk; Moon
Prabal	Strong; Powerful; Mighty; Great
Prabhas	Splendor; Beauty
Prabhu	Excelling; Surpassing; Powerful; Mighty; Strong
Prabuddha	Awakened; Clear sighted; Wise; Learned; Expanded; Unfolded
Prachit	To know; Make known; Appear; Announce
Pradeep	Light; Kindle; Blaze; Fire; Flame

Pradyu	Good work leading to heaven; Works secure heaven
Pradyumna	Pre-eminently mighty one; Son of Krishna
Pradyut	Shining; Brilliant
Pragnhan	Prudent; Wise; Clever; Learned; Knowledge; Wisdom; Intelligence
Praharsha	Extremely joy; Hilarity; Mirth; Gladness; Delight; Exult
Prahlad	Delighted; Rejoiced; Pleased; Happiness
Prajval	Burning; Shining; Epithet of the Sun; Blaze; Light; Fire
Prakarsh	Eminence; Excellence; Perfection; Merit; Superiority
Prakash	Light; Shine; Glitter; Illuminate; Irradiate
Prakasya	Object revealed or illumined
Prakat	Evident; Clear; Manifest; Apparent
Prakat	Manifest; revealed
Praket	Intelligence; One who knows everything; Perception; Appearance
Pramad	Joyful; Pleasure; Delight
Pramey	Object of proof; subject of enquiry; object of right knowledge; measured or known object

Pramod	Excessively joy; Delight; Pleasure; Gladness
Pramod	The pleasure which one gets through the actual enjoyment of an object
Pramud	Pleased; Happy; Gladness; Delight; Pleasure
Pranav	Praise; Sacred Om; Small drum
Pranay	Leading; Guiding; Confidence; Trust; Leader; Friendship; Kindness
Praneet	Conduct; Leading; Guidance; favour
Pranshu	Great Stature; High; Tall; Lofty
Pranut	Praised; Celebrated; Lauded
Prasad	Contend; Satisfied; Glad; Gracious; propitious; Calm; Appeased
Prashant	Calm; Composed; Tranquillized; Divinity
Pratap	Shine; Glow; Kindle; Light; Illumine
Pratik	Turned towards; Directed towards; Outward firm or shape
Pratik	An image or symbol of God for worship and spiritual contemplation
Pratish	Receive; Follow; Attend; Observe; Obey
Pratyabhigna	Knowing; recognition or recovering consciousness; recollection

Praveen	Skillful; Clever; Proficient; Conversant; Versed
Pravid	Possess Knowledge; Wisdom; Understand
Pravir	Heroic; Strong; Powerful; Excellent; Warrior
Prayas	Pleasure; Enjoyment; Delight
Preet	Pleasurable sensation; Pleasure; Joy; Gladness; Happiness; Enjoyment
Prem	Love; Affection; Kind; Tender; Regard; Favour
Preyas	Dearer; Very dear; More agreeable; More desirable; More beloved; Kinder
Prithivi	The Earth; Earth personified
Priyadarshan	Pleasant or grateful to sight; Good looking; Handsome; Lovely
Pulakit	Bristling up with Joy; Thrilled with joy; Delighted; Rejoiced; Enraptured
Purnoham	I am full, the absolute, the infinite; I am Brahman
Bhairav	An epithet of Shiva
Bhargav	Good archer; Epithet of Shiva
Bhaskar	The Sun; Light-causing; Shining; Glittering; Resplendent; Epithet of Shiva
Bhasu	The Sun

Bhasvar	Shining; Radiant; Brilliant; Bright; Bright; Resplendent
Bhasya	To be brought to light; To be made visible
Bhuma	The unconditioned; infinite; Brahma
Bhushan	Decorating; Adorning; Embellishment; Epithet of Vishnu
Bhushit	Decorated; Ornamented; Embellished; Garnished
Bhuvan	Being; Living; World; Mankind; The heaven; The earth; Bring into existence
Bhuvan	World
Bimba	Original
Bodha	Spiritual wisdom; knowledge; intelligence
Brahma	God as creator; the first of the created beings
Buddha	Enlightened; Completely conscious; Understood; Awaken
Buddha	The enlightened one; full of knowledge
Buddhi	Perception; Observation; Intelligence; Mind; Wisdom
Buddhi	Intellect; understanding; reason
Madan	Passion; Love; Embrace; Delighting; Maddening
Madhur	Sweet; Honey; Pleasant; Attractive; Melodious

Madhur	The attitude of a devotee expressing the emotion
Mahan	The Great; the evolute from Prakriti according to the Sankhya
Mahant	Great; Large; king
Maharshi	Great sage
Mahat	Great; the first product from Prakriti in evolution according to Sankhya philosophy, intellect
Mahatma	Great soul; saint; sage
Māhendra	God Indra; The rainbow
Mahesh	The great lord; The great god; Epithet of Shiva
Mahesvar	Great Lord; name of Siva
Māhesvar	God Shiva; Worshiping Shiva
Māheya	The Earth; Son of the Earth
Mahi	The Great world; Earth; Soil; Ground
Mahir	The Sun; The King
Mahit	Honoured; celebrated; Revered; Esteemed
Maitreya	Friendly; Friend; Benevolent; Buddha
Makarand	Juice or Nectar of Flowers; The honey of flowers

Manan	Thoughtful; Careful; Reflection; Intelligence; understanding
Manan	Constant thinking; reflection; meditation on the eternal verities
Manas	Intellect; Intelligence; Understanding; Sense; Conscience; Will
Manas	Mind; the thinking faculty
Mangal	Happiness; Felicity; Good fortune; Good luck; Success; Prosperity; Bliss
Manish	Independent power of thinking
Manu	Thought; Mental faculty; Sacred; Prayer; Incarnation; Spell
Martand	The Sun; Sun god; Aditya; Preceptor
Martand	The Sun-God
Marut	A certain class of heavenly bodies; the wind-god
Mauli	The Head; The top of anything
Mayur	Peacock; Name of a poet; Name of Mountain
Mitra	Companion; Associate; Friend; The Sun
Modit	Pleased; Gratified; Delighted
Mohan	Fascinating; Infatuated; Depriving of Consciousness or sensation
Mohin	Illusive; Fallacious; Alluring; Fascinating

Mohit	Illusion; Fascinating; Infatuated; Perplexed
Mrityunjay	Overcoming death; Death conqueror; Epithet of Shiva
Mudit	Complacency; joy
Mukul	Soul; Spirit; Bud; Flower; King
Mukunda	Giver of liberation; Epithet of Vishnu
Muni	To think; Perceive; Holy man; Devine; Ascetic; Devotee; Monk
Murari	Enemy of Mura; Epithet of Krishna
Mūrti	Embodiment; Manifestation; Incarnation; Air; Fire; Water; Visible shape
Yakshat	Worship; Honour; Reverence
Yuvan	Young; youthful; Natural strength; Strong; Healthy; Agni; Indra
Rachit	Made; Formed; Produced; Made ready; Composed; Written; Decorated
Rāhul	Affectionate; Conqueror of miseries
Rājeev	Living like King
Rajisht	Most Honest; Upright
Rakshit	Guarded; Protected; Taken care
Raman	Pleasing; Gratifying; Delighting; Rejoicing

Rana	Joy; Delight; Gratification; Pleasure; Motion; Battle; Combat
Ratan	Pleased; Delighted; Gratified; Satisfied; Happy
Revant	Son of Surya (The Sun)
Rishabh	Excellent; Eminent; Young Bull; Epithet of Lord Shiva
Rishi	Praiser; Sage; One invoke deities
Rita	Honest; Brave; Competent; Respected; Enlightened
Ritu	Worship; Right time; Right season
Ritvik	Priest performing a sacrifice
Rochak	Brightening; Enlightening; Pleasing; Agreeable
Rochak	Pleasure-inducing
Rohan	Raising; Mounting; Standing on; Healing
Rohin	Raising; Mounting up; Growing; Long; Tall
Rohit	The Sun; Deer; Epithet of Rivers
Lalit	Cheerful; Handsome; Elegant; Pleasant
Lilamay	A connotative name of the divine force
Vāhita	Exerted; Efforted; Endeavored; Mystified

Vaibhav	Supreme human power or might; Greatness; Majesty; Grandeur; Wealth; Glory
Vaishnav	Worshiping Vishnu; Belong to Vishnu; Modern Hindu sect
Vallabh	Beloved; Desire; Dear; Supreme; Lover; Friend; Favorite
Varāha	Lord Vishnu incarnation; Wild bear; Superiority; Pre-eminence
Varchas	Vital power; Energy; Vigour; Efficacy; The Sun
Varchāsya	Bestowing vital power or vigour
Vardha	Act of Increasing; Prosperity; Happy; Strengthening
Vardhan	Increasing; Augmenting; Bestowing prosperity
Vārshneya	An epithet of Krishna; Descendant Vishnu
Varun	Universal encompassed; All enveloper; King of all gods and universe
Varun	The divine intelligence presiding over the element of water
Vasan	Subtle desire; a tendency created in a person by the doing of an action or by enjoyment
Vasanth	To shine; Spring season
Vāsav	Name of Indra
Vasu	Good; Wealthy; Rich; Sweet

Vatsala	Affectionate; kind; Loving; Tender; fond of
Vatsalya	Affectionate towards children; Fond of children
Venkat	Name of a mountain; King; Lord of Venkata mountain; Deity
Vibhav	Power; Might; Supreme power; Property; Wealth; Magnanimity
Vibhu	All-pervading; great
Vibhū	Arise; Prevail; Expand; Reveal; Power
Vibhuti	Manifestation; divine glory and manifestation of divine power
Vibodh	Awakening; Perceiving; Observing; Intelligence; Unfolding
Vibudh	Learned; Wise; Teacher; Pandit; Immortal; God; The Moon
Vibushan	Decoration; Ornaments; Glittering with ornaments
Vighnesh	The god who removes obstacles
Vignan	The principle of pure intelligence
Vignesh	Lord Ganesh
Vigneya	To be perceived; Known; Understood; Cognizable; Intelligible; Comprehensible
Vihā	Heaven; Paradise; Sky
Vihag	Sky-goer; A bird; A cloud; The Sun; The Moon; The planet

Viharsha	Great joy; Pleasure; Gladness
Vihas	Laugh gently; Smile
Vijay	Conquest; Victorious; Overcome; Overpower; Win
Vijit	Conquered; Subdued; Defeated; Won; Gained
Vikas	The Moon; Expanding; Opening; Glowing
Vikram	To step beyond; To pass beyond; To advance; To show velour or prowess
Vikrant	Displaying prowess, valiant; Victorious; A hero; Victor
Vilās	Merriness; Pastime; Play; Dalliness; Grace; Elegance; Charm; Beauty
Vilāsin	Sportive; Playful; Dallying; Fire; Moon; Epithet of Vishnu, Krishna
Vilohit	An epithet of Rudra; Fire; Deep red or purple colour
Vimal	Pure; Clean; Transparent; Beautiful
Vinand	Joyful; Rejoice; Be glad
Vinay	Leading; Guiding; Moral training; Discipline; Decency; Modesty; Humility
Vinay	Humility or sense of propriety; manners
Vinīt	Well trained; Well educated; Disciplined; Modest; Virtuous

Vinod	Pleasure; Enjoyment; Gratification; Eagerness; Vehemence
Vipul	Abundant; Deep; Profound; Plenty
Viraj	Free from Rajas or passion
Virāj	Shining; Radiant; Splendor; Beauty; Epithet of Vishnu
Virat	The physical world that we see; the Lord
Virinchi	Name of Brahma, Vishnu, Shiva
Viruch	To shine forth; Glitter; Bright; Radiant; Eminent; Famous
Virupaksha	Diversely eyed; Epithet of Shiva
Vishāl	Large; Great; Eminent; Illustrious
Vishank	Fearless; Undaunted; Fearlessly
Vishast	Praised; Celebrated
Vishna	Lustre; Splendor
Vishnu	All pervading; Encompassing; Lord Vishnu
Vishrav	Great fame; Celebrity
Vishva	Universe; God of everything, Indra
Vishvak	Name of Sage; All pervading; Universal

Vishvas	Trust; Confident; Faith
Vishvat	Everywhere; All pervade
Visva	Cosmos; a name of the Jiva in the waking state
Visvak-sen	Whose powers go everywhere; Lord Vishnu
Visvarup	Cosmic form; multiform having all forms
Visvas	Faith
Vivardhan	Act of Increasing; Prosperity; Powerful; Advancing
Vivas	Shine forth; Shine; Sunrise
Vivasvat	The brilliant one; The Sun
Vivechak	The separator; Epithet of Agni
Vivek	Discrimination (truth from untruth); Judgement; True knowledge
Vivrit	Uncover; Unfold; Discover; Manifest; Evident; Expound
Viyat	Sky; Heaven; Atmosphere
Vobodhit	Awakened; Aroused; To perceive; To know; Instructed
Vyas	The name of a great sage who wrote the Brahma Sutras
Sabhājit	Served; Honoured; Treated with courtesy; Gratified; Pleased

Sachetan	Possessed of consciousness
Sadachar	Right conduct
Samanyu	Having same splendor; Same energy; Epithet o Shiva
Samarth	Having proper aim or force; Very forcible; Adequate; Well suited; Very powerful
Samharsha	Delight; Joy; Pleasure; Emulation; Thrill
Samīkshit	To behold; Perceive; Consider; Mind
Samīr	Cause to move; Excited; Revive; Confer; Bestow; Wind; Air
Samit	Sacrificial fuel
Sampad	Success; Prosperity; Good fortune
Sampat	Perfection; wealth; virtue
Sampāt	Meeting together; Flying together; Concurrence
Samprasad	Peace; serenity; calmness; tranquillity
Samprayog	Contact of the senses with the objects
Samprit	Completely satisfied; Pleased; Delighted
Samud	To look; To perceive; To look up to one
Samvit	Knowledge; consciousness; intelligence

Sanand	With bliss
Sanat	Bestowing; Granting; Name of Brahma
Sandesh	Communication of intelligence, Information, tidings, news
Sandīp	Shine very brightly; Glow; Light up; Kindle; Inflame; Excite; Encourage
Sandrishy	Having looked at; Having seen, observed, perceived
Sanit	Granted; Gained; Obtained
Sanjay	To conquer together; To gain; Conquered entirely
Sanjit	Completely conquering, winning
Sanjīv	Live together; To live with; Revive; Exist; Restore to life
Sanket	Indicatory sign; Agreement; Convention; Condition; Provision
Santosh	Satisfaction; Contentedness; Happiness; Delight; Joy; Pleasure
Sārthak	Having meaning; Full of meaning; Important; Serviceable; Useful
Sāttvik	Natural; Genuine; True; Honest; Virtuous; Excellent; Vigorous; Energetic
Shachisth	Strong; Most powerful; Very powerful
Shāktik	Worshiper of the Shakti; Personification of divine energy
Shākya	Buddha; Name of the family of Buddha; Buddhist ascetic

Sham	Happiness; Welfare; Prosperity; Blessing; Beauty; Health
Shāmbhav	Belong to Shiva; Worshipper of Siva
Shambhu	Belong to Shiva; Worshipper of Siva
Shankar	Causing happiness; Conferring good fortune, prosperity; Epithet of Shiva
Shantanu	The king of lunar dynasty
Sharad	Autumn; Season of autumn
Sharanyu	Protector; Defender
Shardūl	A Tiger; Eminent person; Best; Excellent
Sharman	Blessing; Happiness; Delight; Pleasure
Sharmay	Grant happiness; Confer prosperity
Sharva	Name of a Vedic deity; Name of Shiva
Shikhar	Point; Peak; Top; Summit; Pinnacle
Shiva	Auspicious; Prosperous; Happy; Fortune; Lucky; Lord Shiva
Shobhan	Adorning; Causing to look beautiful; Shining; Splendid; Epithet of Shiva
Shobit	Beautiful; Adorned; Decorated; Splendid

Shrāvan	The act of Hearing; Knowledge from hearing; Fame; Glory; Wealth; Asterism
Shravas	The ear; Fame; Renown; Glory; Wealth
Shreyansh	Best; Most excellent; Eminent; Illustrious; Prosperous
Shreyas	Most excellent; Superior; Preferable; Best; Very fortunate; Prosperous; Moral; Merit
Shri	Prosperity; Well-being; Wealth; Happiness; Fortune; Success
Shriyas	Happiness; Prosperity; Ornament; Decorated
Shukla	Light; Bright; White; White colour; The Moon; Epithet of Shiva
Siddhārth	Accomplished; Successful; Prosperous; Epithet of great Buddha
Sravan	Hearing of the Srutis or scriptures; ear
Sreyas	Good; blessedness; Moksha
Sukrit	Doing good; benevolent; Virtuous; Pious; Learned; Fortunate
Sukrit	Good act; merit
Susil	One whose nature is purified
Svādhis	Well minded; Thoughtful; Contemplative; Meditating
Svadhit	Well read; Well versed in or conversant with
Svanik	Having beautiful lustre; Very radiant; Agni

Svaran	Illustrious; Celebrated
Hari	Name of Vishnu, Krishna; The Moon; The Sun
Harish	Joyful; Happiness
Harsha	Thrilled; enraptured; Rejoiced; Delighted; Glad
Hriday	Heart; essential center

Made in the USA
Monee, IL
27 February 2025